D1568367

Landmark
Events in
American
History

The California
Missions

Dale Anderson

WORLD ALMANAC® LIBRARY

Please visit our web site at: www.worldalmanaclibrary.com
For a free color catalog describing World Almanac® Library's list of high-quality
books and multimedia programs, call 1-800-848-2928 (USA) or 1-800-387-3178
(Canada). World Almanac® Library's fax: (414) 332-3567.

Library of Congress Cataloging-in-Publication Data

Anderson, Dale, 1953-
    The California missions / by Dale Anderson.
      p. cm. — (Landmark events in American history)
    Summary: Describes the arrival of the Spanish in early California, their impact
on the native inhabitants, and the founding and construction of missions there to
support their claim on the land.
    Includes bibliographical references and index.
    ISBN 0-8368-5339-3 (lib. bdg.)
    ISBN 0-8368-5353-9 (softcover)
    1. Missions, Spanish—California—History—Juvenile literature. 2. California—
History—To 1846—Juvenile literature. 3. Indians of North America—Missions—
California—Juvenile literature. 4. Indians, Treatment of—California—History—
Juvenile literature. 5. Franciscans—Missions—California—History—Juvenile
literature. [1. Missions, Spanish—California—History. 2. California—History—
To 1846.] I. Title. II. Series.
F864.A53 2002
979.4—dc21   2002023495

This North American edition first published in 2002 by
World Almanac® Library
330 West Olive Street, Suite 100
Milwaukee, WI 53212 USA

This U.S. edition © 2002 by World Almanac® Library.

Produced by Discovery Books
Editor: Sabrina Crewe
Designer and page production: Sabine Beaupré
Photo researcher: Sabrina Crewe
Maps and diagrams: Stefan Chabluk
World Almanac® Library editorial direction: Mark J. Sachner
World Almanac® Library art direction: Tammy Gruenewald
World Almanac® Library production: Susan Ashley

Photo credits: Corbis: cover, pp. 4, 5, 10, 17, 26, 31, 32, 34, 37, 41, 42, 43; Granger
Collection: pp. 9, 19, 20, 21, 22, 36, 38; Library of Congress: pp. 8, 11, 12, 13, 14, 15
North Wind Picture Archives: pp. 16, 18, 24, 25, 27, 28, 29, 30, 35, 39; Northwestern
University Library: p. 7; San Fernando Valley Historical Society: p. 40.

Printed in the United States of America

1 2 3 4 5 6 7 8 9 06 05 04 03 02

Contents

Introduction

The Mission Buildings

Along the coast of California is a string of twenty-one beautiful buildings, most of which were constructed more than two hundred years ago. These are the **missions**, and each one was once a complex of church, living quarters, and workplace.

An Empire in America

Until the mid-1700s, California had been inhabited only by the Native people of the region. In 1769, however, the Spanish **Empire** in North America spread from Mexico and the Southwest into California. This was when the California mission system was founded by Spanish priests and soldiers who came to California from Mexico.

The mission of San Carlos Borroméo de Carmelo was founded in 1770. It became the headquarters of the mission system in California.

The Coming of the Missions

The missions heralded the beginnings of Spanish culture in California and, in many ways, the end of Native cultures that had existed for thousands of years. The Spanish took control of the area to acquire wealth for themselves, keep out other European powers, and impose their religion and ways of life on the Native population.

The missions were built and worked on by several generations of Native Americans forced to toil under the direction of Spanish **friars**. They quickly became the economic centers of this Spanish **colony**, with many missions turning into productive farms, ranches, and workshops.

The missionaries also succeeded in their aim of bringing Spanish culture to California, a strong and lively culture that endures today. Many California cities began as missions during this period, which is why the cities still carry the names of saints (*san* and *santa* are Spanish for male and female saint). Unfortunately, the missions were also responsible for the enslavement and deaths of most of the Native people in the southern and mid-coast areas of California.

In the church of the Santa Barbara mission, a painted statue of St. Barbara looks down from the altar. All the California missions were named after patron saints.

Pioneers of the Pacific Coast

"We were the pioneers of the Pacific coast, building towns and missions while General Washington was carrying on the war of the Revolution, and we often talk together of the days when a few hundred large Spanish ranches and mission tracts occupied the whole country from the Pacific to the San Joaquin [valley]. . . . We try, as best we may, to honor the founders of our ancient families, and the saints and heroes of our [early] history."

Guadalupe Vallejo, who grew up on a ranch in California, Ranch and Mission Days in Alta California, *1890*

Chapter 1

The Native Peoples of California

No one knows when the first people reached the place we now call California, but archaeological evidence makes it clear that people were living in the area at least ten thousand years ago. Many different Native groups lived in California before Europeans came. Each group had its own territory and took advantage of the **resources** available in its area.

The Regional Groups

Mountainous northwestern California had plenty of trees, which people felled by using fire and wedges made from elk horns. They

This map shows where different groups of Native Californians lived until the region was settled by Europeans.

turned those trees into planks to build houses or made them into dugout canoes to use for fishing. Each fall, people in this area celebrated with a ceremony called the "World Renewal." They appealed to the spirits for protection from disasters such as earthquakes or famine.

Many people in the northern and northeastern parts of the state lived on high land that had few resources. One resource was abundant, however: a plant called tule, which is a reed that grows tall in marshy areas. The peoples of these regions wove the long tule leaves into floor mats and coverings for their shelters.

Numerous groups occupied the central part of California. Food was plentiful in the region, and for this reason, the area was well populated. Some groups lived in large villages that held as many as one thousand people. Peoples of the central coast—such as the Costanoan and Salinan—later became part of the mission system.

Most of the missions were in Southern California. This region was home to coastal peoples such as the Chumash, Diegueño, and Tongva (or Gabrieleño), who made wooden boats that they used to harvest plants and animals from the ocean.

Two Important Foods

Two foods were especially important protein sources for most Native Californians: salmon and acorns. Salmon were fished from the rivers that flowed to the Pacific Ocean. Acorns were gathered and ground down into a coarse flour that could be either baked or cooked into a mixture similar to grits.

Food Supply

The Native people of California were hunters and gatherers. They lived in one area during the entire year, exploiting the many plant and animal foods that could be found there. Food in many parts of California was abundant, often allowing people to gather more than they needed and store the extra.

Many Native people in California practiced basket making. The baskets had practical uses, for storage and sorting grain, but they were also woven in beautiful designs, such as these photographed by Edward Curtis.

Native Californian fishermen used a combination of lines and nets to catch salmon in the rivers flowing into the Pacific Ocean.

Men hunted and fished, while women gathered foods such as nuts and berries. Food gatherers made their own tools for the various tasks.

In some areas, such as the hot deserts of the southeastern part of the state, fewer resources were available. People living there found other foods, gathering pine nuts and mesquite beans and hunting small game. Those in the northern and northeastern areas ate the bulbs of the tule plants that were so plentiful there. People in other regions supplemented salmon and acorn by hunting elk and deer.

Only the Yuma people of the far southeast corner farmed. Wild foods were plentiful enough to make farming unnecessary for groups living in other parts of California.

Trade Networks

Native cultures across the Americas had extensive trade networks, and those who lived in California were no exception. Each group traded the resources that it

Early Encounter

"The women are very beautiful and virtuous, the children are fair and blonde and very merry. . . . .The people are] affable, generous Indians, friendly to the point of giving whatever they had; they much regretted the Spaniards' departure, because they had so much affection."

Unknown chronicler describing people encountered during an expedition along the Californian coast in 1602, led by Spanish explorer Sebastian Vizcaino

had in abundance for goods that it lacked. The cultures of northeastern California, for instance, mined the rock **obsidian,** which was highly valued for making blades. Coastal people traded fish and shellfish. One group mined soapstone, which was carved into containers and cooking implements. Other groups traded medicinal plants and woven baskets.

Society in Native California

Most people in California lived in small groups and small areas with fewer people, less land, and fewer political alliances between groups than in most other parts of North America. Some scholars have named such groups "tribelets." These groups tended to include only a few hundred or a few thousand people and could occupy a territory as small as 50 square miles (130 square kilometers).

The members of each group were tightly bound to each other. Groups were headed by chiefs, who usually inherited their positions from their fathers. Chiefs were generally males, but the Pomo and some other groups had female chiefs who may have served along with male leaders. Chiefs had the power to make many decisions, including when the group should gather food and who should carry out the work. They also controlled any extra food supplies or other resources, which they doled out when needed.

These chiefs had the highest status in the group and often dressed in special clothes that reflected their position. They did not lead alone, however. Groups had councils—comprising the heads of each extended family—that advised the chief.

This house of a Diegueño woman, photographed by Edward Curtis, was a traditional dwelling in California. Dried grasses were woven into a frame made of wooden poles.

What Happened to the Original Californians?

About 300,000 Native Americans lived in California when the Spaniards arrived. This number was halved between 1770 and the 1840s, when people were wiped out by diseases like measles and smallpox that came from Europe. The people of California had no resistance to these diseases. The mission system, in which people were forced into labor and terrible living conditions, also took its toll, killing many thousands of Native Californians.

Worse followed when the United States took over California in 1848. Gold was found there in that same year, and thousands of **prospectors** came seeking their fortune. Many of these white settlers roamed the area in gangs, killing any Native people they found; thousands died at their hands. During the rest of the 1800s, many more Indians died due to brutality, disease, and causes associated with their poverty. By 1900, there were fewer than sixteen thousand Native Americans in California.

Chapter 2

The Spanish in the Americas

Arrival of the Spanish

The founding of the missions in California was part of a huge change that occurred in the world when Europeans colonized the Americas. That change began taking place in 1492 when Christopher Columbus first sailed to the Caribbean Sea.

Spanish explorations were partly fueled by religious fervor. When Spaniards entered Tenochtitlán, the capital of the Aztecs in central Mexico, they pulled down the Aztecs' religious statues and replaced them with Christian ones of their own. They repeated these actions across the Americas, always looking for more and more people to convert—usually by force—to Christianity.

Gold and Glory

Many Spaniards who came to the Americas were willing to undergo hardships in the hopes that they could find gold. They also wanted to make a name for themselves. They braved long voyages and strange climates and initiated fierce fighting because they believed that they could win fame and honor for themselves and their families. Gold and glory, therefore, were two other factors that motivated Spaniards in their quest for an empire in the Americas.

Dedicated to God

"God made me the messenger of the new heaven and the new earth of which he spoke in the Apocalypse of St. John after having spoken of it through the mouth of the prophet Isaiah; and he showed me the post where to find it."

Christopher Columbus, in a letter about his explorations, 1498

When the explorer Hernán Cortés led his forces into Tenochtitlán in 1519, the Spanish struck gold. Within two years, the Spaniards had conquered the Aztecs with their violence, weapons, and cruelty, gaining great wealth for themselves and for Spain. In the 1530s, Francisco Pizarro encountered the Inca empire of South America. He captured the emperor Atahualpa and was offered gold as a ransom. Once he had the gold, Pizarro had the emperor killed and proceeded to conquer his empire, gaining even larger supplies of gold and silver.

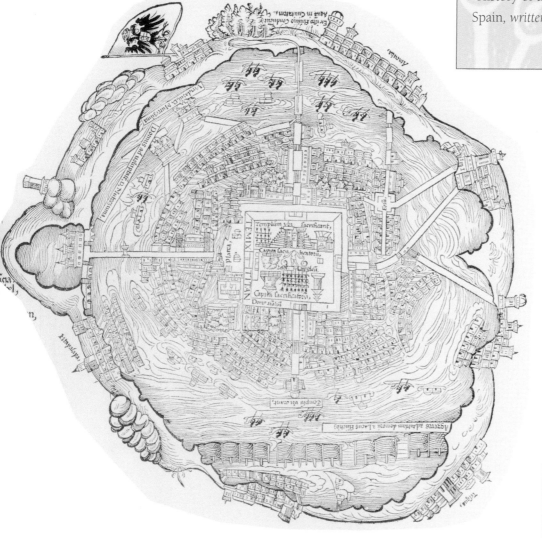

The Aztec capital of Tenochtitlán was a magnificent center with over 300,000 inhabitants, huge buildings, and flourishing trade and industries. This map of the city was sent to Spain by Hernán Cortés to impress the Spanish king. The original drawing was given to Cortés by the Aztec people between 1519 and 1521.

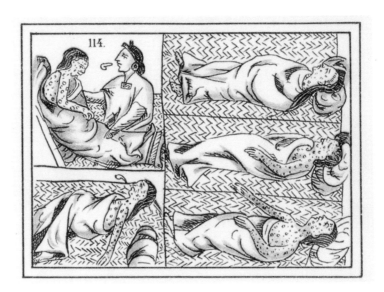

Native people had no resistance to diseases, such as smallpox, brought by the Spanish. As a result, they died in large numbers. This sixteenth-century drawing illustrated a report by a Spanish priest and is one of the few early images to depict the suffering of Native Americans.

Looking Further Afield

The Spaniards pushed from Mexico and Peru into new areas and began planting colonies. In 1565, the colony of St. Augustine was founded in Florida, and in 1598, Juan de Oñate started a new Spanish colony near modern Santa Fe, New Mexico. These areas remained on the fringes of the Spanish Empire, however. South America, Mexico, and the Caribbean held the important colonies.

Enslaving Native Americans

The Native Americans who lived within these core areas suffered terribly. The Europeans had brought new diseases, like smallpox and measles, that killed tens of thousands of people.

Hard, forced labor killed many more. The Spaniards turned Native Americans into slaves, forcing them to work so that they themselves could live in leisure. Slaves mined gold and silver and did all the farming and ranching. They suffered from overwork, from whippings for refusal to work, from every kind of abuse imaginable.

The Suffering of the Native Americans

"[The Native Americans were] without fraud, without subtlety or malice . . . toward the Spaniards whom they serve, patient, meek and peaceful.

"To these quiet Lambs . . . came the Spaniards like most cruel tigers, wolves, and lions, enraged with a sharp and tedious hunger; for these forty years past, minding nothing else but the slaughter of these unfortunate wretches, whom with diverse kinds of torments neither seen nor heard of before, they have so cruelly and inhumanely butchered."

Spanish priest Bartolomé de Las Casas, Brief Report on the Destruction of the Indians, *1542*

Bartolomé de Las Casas (1474—1566)

Bartolomé de Las Casas was born in Spain and began his career as a soldier. In 1502, Las Casas joined an expedition to the Americas and received a grant of land in the Caribbean. By 1513, Las Casas had become a priest. In 1515, he went back to Spain to try to persuade the king to end Indian slavery.

Las Casas believed strongly in his duty to ensure the salvation of Native people. They could only be saved if they could be converted to Christianity, however, and they could not be converted if they continued to die. In 1520, Las Casas won the Crown's approval for a plan to found a model colony of farmers and free Indians in what is now Venezuela. When the attempt failed, Las Casas began writing about the mistreatment of Indians. Even after King Charles I agreed to end Indian slavery in 1542, Las Casas continued to campaign on behalf of Native Americans. He died in Spain at age ninety-two.

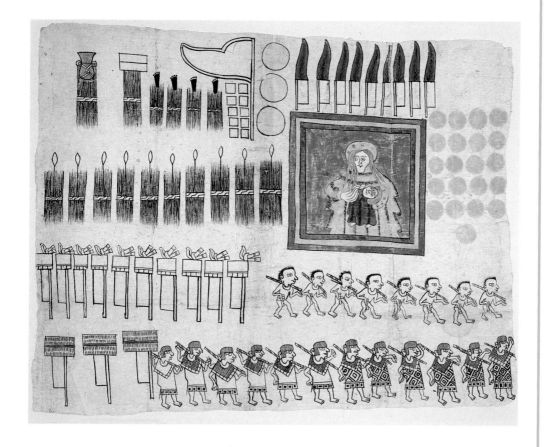

A page from a 1531 legal document sent to the Spanish authorities by the people of Huexotzinco, Mexico, to protest unfair taxes and labor. The drawing shows the products and services provided by Native people to the Spanish. These surround an image of Mary and Jesus.

15

The settlement of Santa Fe was founded by the Spanish in 1609 as the capital of New Mexico. This building in Santa Fe is believed to be the oldest Spanish building in the United States. The drawing shows it as it was in the 1800s.

Competing for Power

Spain's success in the Americas encouraged other European nations to try to secure colonies and riches of their own. The British planted colonies along the Atlantic seaboard from present-day Maine to Georgia and in the Caribbean. France, meanwhile, took control of the St. Lawrence River, the Great Lakes, and the Mississippi River.

The French advance down the Mississippi Valley put the Spanish hold on Texas in danger and prompted Spain to start settlements north of Mexico. In the 1700s, however, few Spaniards were willing to move from the well-established colonies in Mexico to the northern lands in what are now the U.S. states of New Mexico, Arizona, and Texas. In order to achieve settlement and control, Spain decided to send small groups of soldiers and a few friars to these areas to found missions. They would force Native people to build and maintain them and convert the inhabitants of the area both to Christianity and to Spanish ways of life. By the middle 1700s, a few missions had been established.

The Spanish Claim on California

This effort did not reach California, or at least not yet. The first European voyage to California, in the 1540s, had been led by Juan Rodríguez Cabrillo. He sailed up the coast, reaching a point north of present-day San Francisco, but he and his men found no riches. As a result, Spanish officials dismissed the expedition as worthless. Nevertheless, Cabrillo had claimed the land for Spain.

In the 1600s, Spain planted settlements and missions in Baja (meaning "lower") California, the **peninsula** that is now part of Mexico. But the Spaniards had little interest in settling what they called Alta (meaning "higher") California, now the state of California. They viewed it as too far away from Mexico.

The Arrival of the Russians

That view changed in the middle 1700s. Russian fur traders had for years been catching seals and sea otters in the northern Pacific Ocean. In the 1750s, they began to move into the waters off the coast of northern California.

Suddenly, Spanish interest in California became more intense. Orders came from Spain "to guard the dominions from all invasion and insult." The king's order to defend the empire was passed down to José de Gálvez, a colonial official in Mexico. Gálvez wanted to organize all the lands north of Mexico into one large area. He saw the king's order as an opportunity for him to carry out his plan.

When the Spanish first arrived in Baja California, they thought it was an island. They named it California after a mythical, enchanted island described in a Spanish novel that was popular in the 1500s. This map reflects the Spanish view of California and Mexico in the 1700s.

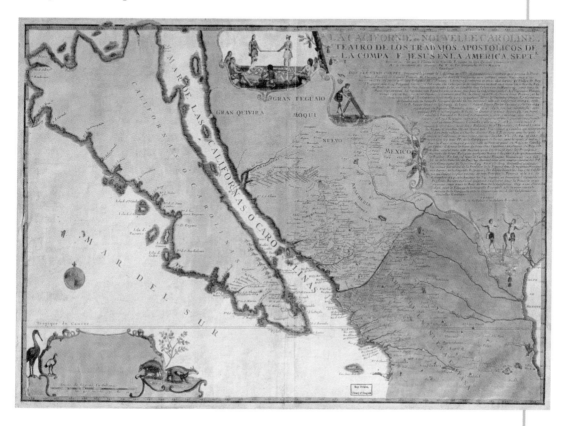

Chapter 3

The Founding of the Missions

The Plan of José de Gálvez

José de Gálvez decided to make missions the centerpiece of the new colony he envisaged in North America. Missions were useful in several ways. First, they were funded by the Catholic Church and not by the Spanish government, and this saved money for the Crown. Second, it was difficult to persuade any Spaniards living in Mexico to move to the unknown land. The way to settle the new colony, Gálvez thought, was to bring in missionaries who would forcibly convert Native Americans to Christianity and European life, as they had done in what is now the state of New Mexico.

On the basis of reports from past explorers, Gálvez hoped to send an expedition to start settlements at the sites of what are now San Diego and Monterey. Both spots were said to have excellent harbors where supplies could arrive by sea.

The Leaders

Two men were chosen to lead the expedition. The military commander was Don Gaspár de Portolá, an experienced officer who volunteered to take charge of the soldiers accompanying the missionaries. The religious leader was the friar Junípero Serra.

The first mission in California was founded at San Diego in 1769. At the mission, a statue of Father Junípero Serra stands on the grounds.

Father Junípero Serra (1713—1784)

Junípero Serra was born on the island of Majorca in Spain. He entered the Catholic Church and advanced quickly, becoming a friar by his twenties and a university teacher by the age of twenty-four. But Father Serra longed for more than teaching. He dreamed of setting up Catholic missions in the Americas. In 1749, he obtained a transfer to Mexico.

In 1768, after years of service in Mexico, Serra was finally named president of the new missions being planned for Alta California. The fifty-five-year-old friar could easily have carried out his duties from a safe distance, living in more settled lands. Instead, he went to California, where, for the next fifteen years, he devoted his energy, his mind, and his faith to the missions.

Today, Serra is a controversial figure. To some he is a hero, and the Catholic Church is even considering whether to name him a saint. But his work took a terrible and fatal toll on the Native people of central and southern California. Serra presumably meant them no harm, and he even wrote once that "if ever the Indians . . . kill me, they should be forgiven." Not only did he contribute to the enslavement of Native people, however, but by today's standards, Serra was a religious and cultural imperialist. This means he was willing to stamp out Native American spiritual beliefs and ways of life because he saw no value in them and thought his own religion and traditions were superior.

The First Mission

The expedition set out from Baja California in early 1769. Four different parties comprising more than two hundred men, nearly all soldiers or priests, were dispatched. Two groups went by sea and two by land. All were to meet at what is now San Diego.

One ship was blown far off course, and the directions that the Spaniards had for San Diego were not accurate. Eventually, members of all four groups reached the right area, but because of death and desertions, only about half the men who had left Baja California reached San Diego.

Father Serra watches as soldiers plant a cross in the ground to mark the founding of the first of the California missions in July 1769.

Less than two weeks after their arrival, Serra planted a cross in the ground and celebrated mass with the men who remained. He declared the site the foundation of the first California mission, San Diego de Alcalá.

Troubles

Portolá, meanwhile, had led a small party of soldiers on a search for Monterey, where the other mission was supposed to be founded. The party was unable to identify Monterey Bay from the descriptions they had, however. After many months and a journey that carried them well north of their goal, Portolá and his men returned to San Diego in January 1770.

Back in San Diego, the Spaniards had built shelters and a crude church. They had also suffered more deaths from disease and from a fight with the Tipai Indians in the area, who attempted to resist this invasion of their territory. In addition, Serra had yet to win a single convert, and the small settlement was growing desperately short of food.

An early view of the San Carlos Borroméo de Carmelo Mission around 1795 shows some of the original **thatched** huts. The early buildings at San Diego would have been similar to these.

The First Presidios

The settlers were saved in March 1770, when a ship arrived with supplies. Portolá erected a small **presidio**, or fort, near the mission. Leaving some of the soldiers in San Diego, Portolá set out the following month to look again for Monterey. He ordered the captain of the ship to carry Serra and another friar by sea to meet him there. Portolá arrived on May 24, and a few days later, the ship anchored in the bay.

Presidios

Presidios were forts where the Spanish posted soldiers to guard their interest against other empire builders. They weren't really big enough or sufficiently well armed to achieve this, but the presidios were at least a symbolic presence. They were also used to protect the missions against Native groups who resisted Spanish intrusion. Unlike the missions that were situated in fertile valleys, the presidios were placed where they could overlook harbors and other strategic spots. They were never self-sufficient, and they relied on the missions, the **pueblos**, and the forced labor of Native people for food.

The presidio at San Francisco in 1816.

After building forts at San Diego and Monterey, the Spanish military in California founded two more presidios to emphasize Spain's presence in California. One was built in 1776 at the northern end of the mission chain, in San Francisco. The other, built in 1782, was in Santa Barbara. All four of the California presidios were originally small, crudely built posts staffed by only a few soldiers.

KEY
† Missions
🏰 Presidios
🏘 Pueblos
— Present day state boundaries

San Rafael Arcángel (1817)
San Francisco de Solano (1823)
San Francisco
San Francisco de Asís (1772)
San José
Santa Clara de Asís (1777)
San José (1797)
Santa Cruz (1791)
Branciforte
San Juan Bautista (1797)
Monterey
San Carlos Borroméo de Carmelo (1770)
Nuestra Señora de Soledad (1791)
San Antonio de Padua (1771)
San Miguel Arcángel (1797)
San Luis Obispo de Tolosa (1772)
La Purísima Concepción (1787)
Santa Inés, Virgin y Martir (1804)
Santa Barbara, Virgin y Martir (1786)
Santa Barbara
San Buenaventura (1782)
San Fernando, Rey de España (1797)
San Gabriel Arcángel (1771)
Los Angeles
San Juan Capistrano (1776)
San Luis, Rey de Francia (1798)
San Diego de Alcalá (1769)
San Diego

PACIFIC OCEAN
NEVADA
CALIFORNIA
MEXICO

N
W E
S

miles
0   100
0   100
km

By 1823, the friars had created a chain of missions along the southern and central California coast stretching from San Diego to north of present-day San Francisco. Four presidios were built to protect Spanish interests. Small towns called pueblos were founded, mainly to supply the presidio soldiers with food.

More Missions

On June 3, Serra founded the second California mission—San Carlos Borroméo de Carmelo. On the same day, Portolá raised the royal flag over a spot that became the presidio of Monterey. The mission, originally next to the presidio, was later moved a few miles away to the more fertile farmland at the mouth of the Carmel Valley, where it was rebuilt in stone.

Over the next fifteen years, Father Serra and his colleagues founded several other missions along the Californian coast. The last in this group, San Buenaventura, was founded by Serra when he was sixty-eight years old.

In 1784, Father Serra died. He was buried in the church at the Carmel mission. Replacing Father Serra was Fermín Francisco de Lasuén, who had done an effective job running the mission at San Diego. Equal to the missions' founder in energy and zeal, Lasuén would lead the missionary effort in Alta California for the next eighteen years.

From 1785 to 1803, Lasuén oversaw the founding of nine more missions. Three additional missions were added to the system after Lasuén's death. One—Santa Inés—filled in a gap in the chain north of Santa Barbara. The last two extended the chain north of San Francisco.

Locating the Missions

As the mission system expanded, so did the Spanish **subjugation** of the Native people. The friars tried to space the missions out so that each had a separate pool of the Native population from which to draw their slave labor and converts. They also looked for fertile areas and plentiful water, usually choosing places already well populated by Native people for the same reasons. Some missions were situated in places that offered other attractions. Santa Barbara, for instance, sits on a hill that provides a beautiful view of the ocean.

Some sites were better than others. San Gabriel flourished so much that it grew to include several hundred thousand acres of farm and ranch land. San José also succeeded, and its lands stretched as far north as present-day Oakland.

Building the Missions

The friars forced Native people living around the chosen sites to perform the actual labor of building the missions. The earliest

The Franciscans sited their missions in some of the most fertile and attractive locations along the Pacific coast. The mission at San Luis Rey boasts orchards and fields that provided produce to feed mission residents and to sell.

buildings were made of wood and given thatch roofs. But thatch was dangerous because the flaming arrows of hostile groups in the area could easily set it on fire. The friars at San Luis Obispo solved the problem by having their roofs made of baked earth, or terra cotta, tiles. This was a practice that other missions copied, and the red tile roofs became part of the distinctive mission style that was based on Spanish traditional architecture.

This photograph of the brickyard at the Santa Barbara mission today shows its typical terra cotta roofs and, in the foreground, the process of making adobe bricks that were used to build the thick mission walls. The bricks were formed in wooden molds from clay, water, manure, and straw and then baked in the sun.

Over time, as the missions became established, more permanent buildings were constructed. Many were made of **adobe** and covered with **stucco**.

"Mission Style"

Renewed interest in the missions in the twentieth century revived the architectural style in California. Architects and builders began to echo the adobe walls covered with stucco, the beamed ceilings and tile roofs, and the gentle arches and curves of the missions as they constructed buildings in booming California. These elements can be seen in many houses being built today.

Another aspect of mission style is seen in furniture. It is a simple design that is now very popular, with straight, flat pieces of wood forming the backs and sides of chairs, table bases, and headboards.

The mission complex consisted of much more than just the church. Other buildings included sleeping quarters for the friars and the workers, storehouses for grain and other supplies, kitchens, and workshops. At many of the missions, the entire complex was built around a central courtyard.

Each mission had a set of bells, used to signal when prayers, work, or meals were to begin. Rather than use bell towers, the friars had their workers construct *campanaria*, which were walls with openings for the bells.

Expansion Beyond the Missions

The friars founded outposts called *asistencias* that were on mission lands but not actual missions, since they had no chapel or resident friar. San Rafael Arcángel began as an asistencia and was used as a hospital for Native people living at San Francisco de Asís. It was a sunnier and drier location, and the health of those sent there rapidly improved. Eventually, San Rafael grew into a bustling community, and in 1823, it became a mission.

The Spanish also established a few towns. Known as pueblos (the Spanish word for village), their purpose was to supply the soldiers at presidios with food. The Spanish government offered free land, animals, and farming supplies to anyone, including Native Americans, who would settle at the pueblos. In return, the settlers would sell their produce to the presidio population. Each pueblo had its own town government and mayor.

The friars placed little importance on material wealth and possessions. Father Serra's room at the Carmel mission, shown here, was no exception to the rule of simple living.

The pueblo of Los Angeles was founded in the San Fernando Valley in 1781. This engraving shows how Los Angeles looked in its early days.

The first pueblo was San José, founded in 1777 by about sixty-five settlers. Next came a pueblo with a very long name—El Pueblo de Nuestra Señora la Reina de los Angeles de Porciúncula. Los Angeles, as it is more commonly known, was founded in 1781 by about forty people. The last pueblo, Branciforte, was built near Santa Cruz. It was set up in 1797 and began with only seventeen settlers.

El Camino Reál

Using the forced labor of local Indians, the Spaniards built the first roadway in California to connect the missions. They called it "El Camino Reál," or "the Royal Road," and it stretched nearly 600 miles (965 km) from the San Diego mission in the south to San Francisco de Solano in the north. This roadway was not as impressive as its name might sound. In an age when people traveled by horseback or oxcart, it was simply a wide dirt path. The Camino Reál was well traveled by soldiers, friars, and traders, however. And it followed a sensible route around California's mountains, a route so practical that modern highways trace the same course.

Life on the Missions

The towns and presidios in California were small. There were also a few Spanish ranches that were independent of the missions, but the missions were the center of life in Spanish California.

The Friars

From the start, there were two friars at each mission. One friar was in charge of religious life and one responsible for overseeing work, although the pair could occasionally switch tasks. The friars had complete control over the lives and labor of the residents. As one mission Indian recalled later in life, "the Fernandino Father is like a king."

Some friars and missions were more humane than others, but many of the friars treated the Native people in their missions as slaves. In fact, all the Native people on the missions were slaves, even the ones who weren't treated cruelly, because they were all forced to work and were not paid for their labor.

A missionary preaches Christianity to a group of Native Americans. This was one method of recruiting new workers for the missions. Harsher methods followed if recruits did not come willingly.

The friars ruled at the missions, not only over the Native laborers but also over the soldiers posted there. Here, soldiers interrupt their card game to show respect to the friar.

The Soldiers

Each mission usually had a small force of soldiers in its compound. Their job was to protect the mission and friars and to enforce obedience among the workers. When an emergency arose, the soldiers sent messages to one of the four presidios to dispatch a larger force. During the mission period, only a few hundred Spanish soldiers served in Alta California at any time.

Recruiting Converts

The friars had two tasks. The first was to take control of the Native people and force them to learn skills and perform tasks—such as crafts or farming—that would make the missions profitable. The aim of the missions was not just to establish a Spanish presence in

Low Opinion

"The Indian in his grave, humble and retired manner, conceals a hypocritical and treacherous disposition. . . . He never looks at any one while in conversation but has a wandering and malicious gaze. For benefits received, he is never grateful. . . . His eyes are never uplifted, but like those of the swine, are cast to the earth. Truth is not in him, unless to the injury of another, and he is exceedingly false."

Father Geronimo Boscana, A Historical Account of the Indians of California, *1825*

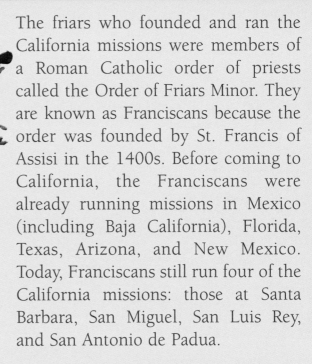

The Franciscans

The friars who founded and ran the California missions were members of a Roman Catholic order of priests called the Order of Friars Minor. They are known as Franciscans because the order was founded by St. Francis of Assisi in the 1400s. Before coming to California, the Franciscans were already running missions in Mexico (including Baja California), Florida, Texas, Arizona, and New Mexico. Today, Franciscans still run four of the California missions: those at Santa Barbara, San Miguel, San Luis Rey, and San Antonio de Padua.

A statue of St. Francis of Assisi in the garden of the San Diego mission.

California, but to make money for Spain. The second task was to convert the local people to Christianity. The converts, or "neophytes," as they were called, were considered to have souls worth "saving," but they were not considered equals in any way.

Potential converts were recruited in various ways. Most were given little choice but to convert. Sometimes, soldiers simply rounded up groups of Native Americans and forced them onto the missions with violence or threats of violence. In other cases, the friars attracted Native people with gifts, or they used tricks. One observer noted that the friars would baptize children, take them into the mission, and deny the parents any contact with the children until they themselves agreed to be baptized.

On other occasions, people came willingly. This may be because they saw the friars as men with powerful connections to

the spirit world, or they may simply have been afraid of what would happen to them if they did not enter the missions. By 1800, thirteen thousand people were living on the missions. There were anything from a few hundred to three thousand people at each site.

Religious Conversion and Suppression

An important job of the friars was to teach Christianity. They gave the people brought into the missions religious instruction and held regular church services.

Of course, the people the friars were trying to convert had their own spiritual beliefs, which they often kept secret. The friars made efforts to stop traditional practices, but some made almost no effort to learn about local beliefs. As one friar commented, "We do not know whether they adore the moon or the sun." However, missionaries recognized that traditional dancing was an important part of the spiritual life of Native Californians, and they did all they could to suppress it.

31

Ranching and Farming

The main work of the missions was farming, and most of the enslaved workers labored in the fields. Men were taught to farm and tend cattle and sheep, and women and children were also forced to do farm work. The laborers raised many crops, including wheat, corn, beans, chick peas, and fruits and vegetables. There were extensive vineyards at some missions, where grapes were grown for wine making. The farm workers also carried out the heavy labor of building dams and ditches for irrigation systems.

As the missions expanded and cattle ranching became a major activity, outlying ranches called *estancias* were built. Native ranch hands were sent to live there, usually with a Spanish overseer in charge.

Learning Crafts

After Lasuén took charge of the mission system, he brought in several skilled craft workers from Mexico to teach metalwork, woodwork, tanning, and stonecutting to male mission laborers.

Because of a lack of skills and materials, the friars could not have columns, decorative metalwork, marble, or other elaborate features in their churches. Instead, they taught their labor force to paint images of these on the walls. This is the restored church at La Purísima mission in Lompoc.

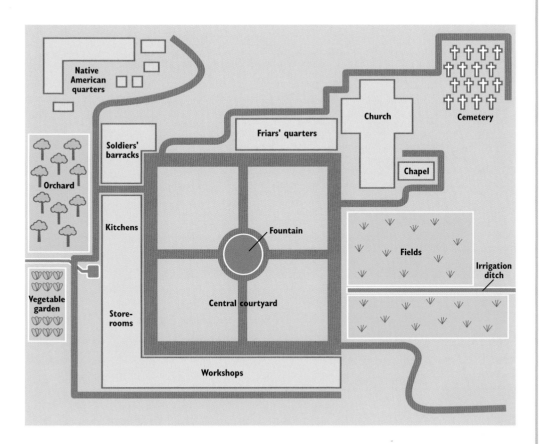

This diagram shows the layout of a typical mission. The complex was usually built around a central courtyard. The missions all had networks of ditches, called *zanjas*, to provide irrigation from nearby rivers to fields, orchards, and vegetable gardens as well as a water supply for the buildings.

Women learned how to weave woolen cloth. The cloth could be dyed with colors extracted from plants, but often it was left in the natural sheep colors of brown, black and white. From this cloth, the women made blankets, shirts, skirts, and breeches for the mission residents and friars and for the soldiers at the presidios. The women also made soap and candles from mission produce.

The Mission Economy

With their large force of slave labor, most of the missions had successful **economies**. By forcing Native people into many tasks, the missionaries built thriving industries. This is most evident in the herds they maintained. By the 1830s, the missions owned thousands of horses and hundreds of thousands of cattle and sheep. The missions became huge, eventually controlling one-sixth of the land in California.

Mission Production
"The products of the mission are butter, **tallow**, hides, chamois [goat] leather, bear skins, wine, white wine, brandy, oil, corn, wheat, beans also bull horns which the English take by the thousand."

Mission Indian Pablo Tac, describing the San Luis Rey mission, 1835

Native people were forced into all kinds of labors to produce money for the missions. On the left, women make baskets, while the group in the middle is spinning rope.

Trade in animals and animal products helped the missions thrive. Lamb and beef could be sold as well as eaten on the missions. In addition, sheep were shorn for wool, and the hides of slaughtered cattle were tanned and turned into leather goods. Beef fat was used to make candles. Some of these goods were used on the missions. Others were traded with the merchants who stopped along the coast to pick up the missions' farm produce and other goods.

Everyday Life

The Native people on the missions were forced to work from dawn to dusk, with breaks for meals. The amount of food given to the Native Americans was meager. In years when grain production was down, the friars did not cut the amount of grain given to the Spanish soldiers, but they did cut back on workers' food. There was no work on Sundays or on the various Catholic feast days during the year, since these days were taken up with religious celebrations and prayer.

At night, parents and children slept in little huts. Single people slept in large dormitories, where males and females were kept separate. The dormitories

Reasons to Run

"He had been [whipped] for leaving without permission."

"He was frightened at seeing how his friends were always being flogged."

"When he wept over the death of his wife and children, he was ordered whipped five times."

"His mother, two brothers, and three nephews died, all of hunger, and he ran away so that he would not also die."

Reasons given by a group of Native Americans for fleeing mission San Francisco de Asís, 1797

were foul-smelling, enclosed places with little light or fresh air. Girls of child-bearing age were taken from their families and put in rooms that were locked at night.

Punishment and Discipline

It was not just the grueling work and grim living conditions that made life so hard, but the way the men, women, and even children were treated by the Spanish. Although the friars were religious people, many did not hesitate to use harsh discipline. Their attitude toward the people in their care was that they required discipline and punishment to become "civilized," and this was reflected in frequent punishments as well as lack of decent care.

A Tongva woman who grew up at San Gabriel later said she saw a mission woman punished by having her head shaved, being whipped every day for fifteen days, wearing iron chains on her feet for three months, and standing on the altar steps every Sunday with a wooden doll in her arms. Her crime was that she had lost a baby by miscarriage. Mission women often tried to end their pregnancies so that their children would not have to grow up in the missions, and so miscarriages were heavily punished by the friars.

Resistance and Escape

Although thousands of Native Americans lived at the missions, resistance was rare. A few people, however, did try to resist the cruelty and slave conditions. San Diego de Alcalá was almost destroyed when the Tipais attacked shortly after it was founded.

This picture shows a mission resident perched high up in the campanaria ringing the bell. Life on the mission was ruled by bells that were rung to summon the Indians to prayers, meals, and work.

The most extreme outbreak of violence came in 1824, when a group of Chumash people seized the missions of Santa Inés and La Purísima Concepción. Soldiers from Monterey arrived on the scene, defeated the rebels, and restored the friars' control.

There is one clear case of a friar dying at the hands of Native Americans, when Father Andrés Quintana was killed at the Santa Cruz mission in 1812 by neophytes. They gave as their reason fear of his cruelty and punishments. In 1801, four friars at different missions fell ill from possible poisoning, and in 1811, a friar at San Diego was reportedly killed with poison by his cook, who had been whipped 124 times in 24 hours.

Every year, as many as 10 percent of the mission residents decided to flee. On some occasions, a few hundred people at a time escaped, hiding as far as possible from the soldiers that the friars sent after them. If they were caught, runaways were placed in the **stocks** or whipped.

This 1786 illustration shows the arrival of Frenchman Jean Francois Galaup de La Perouse at the Carmel mission head-quarters. Perouse was critical of the way the Native Americans were treated there.

Cultural Impact

Native Californians living on the missions adopted some aspects of Spanish culture. They began to wear European-style clothes instead of their traditional scant clothing and learned many skills. Some who fled the missions continued to follow Spanish ways of life, even including Christian symbols in their spiritual practices.

On the other hand, the Indians retained some aspects of their traditional culture because friars could not wipe out the Native social structure. Many Mission Indians just pretended to convert to Christianity in order to be fed and avoid punishment. Despite their persecution and humiliation by the friars, the spiritual leaders and tribal chiefs continued to have influence as a steady flow of new recruits brought traditional practices into the missions and kept them alive.

A group of Californians wearing ceremonial body paint perform a traditional dance. Dancing was among the spiritual and cultural practices that missionaries tried to eradicate.

Devastation of the Californian Peoples

The missions contributed to the devastation of the Native population of California. The friars may not have planned it, but large numbers of people died on the missions. One reason was disease, as outbreaks of smallpox and other diseases took their toll.

There were other reasons, also. The first was that the Mission Indians were weakened by being underfed. Another reason for the high death rate was lack of hygiene that led to breathing problems and stomach problems. Pregnant women and small children were especially vulnerable, and in 1820, a shocking 86 percent of the children born at the missions died in infancy.

Psychological reasons also played a part in the high death rate. Many visitors to the missions commented on how the Indians often seemed without energy and depressed. Some historians think that this depression sapped the Native Americans' will to live.

Chapter 5

The End of the Mission System

New Government and New Ideas

Although the missions were economic successes, the original plan had been to disband each one after ten years. At the end of that time, they were supposed to become pueblos, the residents to become free settlers, and the friars to move on to begin new missions. This never happened. Some people gained "freedom" after ten years but found themselves still under the control of the Spanish. Prejudice against the Native population was strong, and the Spanish never intended for the Native Californians to become equals even when they left the missions.

By the 1820s, Mexico was independent of Spain, and California had become a Mexican **province**. Some Mexican leaders began to discuss the idea of **secularizing** the missions, which would mean taking the land out of the church's hands and giving it to individuals.

The Demand for Mission Lands

Throughout the early 1800s, more people on the missions were dying than were born. As a result, there were fewer and fewer

Vaqueros, or cowboys, round up a steer on a ranch near San Francisco. By the beginning of the nineteenth century, ranching was established in California, and the missions owned large areas of the best ranch land. Spanish settlers in California wanted mission lands for their own ranches.

Miserable as their existence was on the missions, the Mission Indians were reluctant to leave. This was probably because they were rightly mistrustful of their future outside the mission walls.

people to do the farming, ranching, and other work. It was becoming harder to replace the lost workers—there were no longer large groups of Native Americans left to be rounded up for mission labor.

The missions also tied up huge amounts of land. The government had made few grants of land, and the missions often held the richest, most fertile fields. The demand was growing for products from cattle ranching, such as beef, hides, and tallow. Newer settlers arriving in California eyed the mission land hungrily.

Secularization

The first attempt at breaking up the missions came in 1826, when the governor of California, José Echeandía, put forth a plan for gradual secularization. Few Native Americans took up the offer of freedom, however. A few years later, a new governor, José Figueroa, came up with a similar plan. Once again, only a handful of Indians agreed to leave the missions, even though the government offered them land, seed, and tools for farming.

A Kind of Freedom

"Having served ten years in the mission, an Indian may claim his liberty. . . . A piece of ground is then allotted for his support, but he is never wholly free from the [mission], as part of his earnings must still be given to them."

British explorer F. W. Beechy, Narratives of a Voyage to the Pacific and Bering's Strait, *1831*

Rogerio Rocha (18??—1904)

Rogerio Rocha was born at the Mission San Fernando Rey, the son of a Chumash man and a Tongva woman. As a young boy, Rocha was trained and worked as a blacksmith and silversmith. After the missions were secularized in 1834 and the priests left, Rocha and other neophytes continued to live on or near the mission. Over time, Rocha emerged as a leader in the Native community. In accordance with Mexican law, Rocha was given a land grant of a few acres of mission land. In 1885, however, he and his wife were evicted from their home by a land developer. Rocha's wife died from pneumonia that developed as a result of the eviction, but Rocha continued to live in the San Fernando Valley, at first in the mission ruins and then in a canyon above the mission. When he died in 1904, it is likely that he was the last surviving neophyte from the California mission system.

Then the government of Mexico stepped in. Mexico's leaders wanted to offer the mission land for sale to encourage more people to settle in California. In April 1834, Mexico passed a law declaring that all the missions had to be secularized in just four months.

Dividing the Missions

California governor José Figueroa put the law into action. He declared that half the mission's property—land and animals—would be given to Mission Indians. The rest would be controlled by an administrator appointed by the government. The core religious buildings, such as the church and the friars' rooms, were kept by the Catholic Church.

The administrators did not carry out the law as it was written. They made deals with friends and associates, giving them the best land and major shares of the mission livestock. Some Native people did receive land, but many were cheated out of it or sold it to shrewd white settlers. Soon, most of the Mission Indians were landless, forced to take any kind of work. They went from being slaves to forming a class of low-paid laborers for the growing Hispanic and Anglo population.

The Missions Decay

The missions fell into decay. Some of the non-religious buildings were divided up among new property owners, becoming homes, stores, saloons, farms, and stables. Others were abandoned, and people made off with what materials they could, including tiles from mission roofs to cover their own homes.

Weather damaged the buildings as well, and roof timbers and walls rotted and collapsed. Within a few decades, most of the buildings were in ruins. Some of the missions, including Santa Cruz and San José, were destroyed as a result of earthquakes.

Continuing Oppression
"We were at the mercy of the administrator, who ordered us to be flogged whenever and however he took a notion. Pío Pico [governor of California] and those who followed him were despots, and in addition Señor Pico required us to carry our hats in our hands whenever we met him as long as we remained in sight."

Julio Cesar, a former Mission Indian, remembering life after secularization, 1839

The missions fell into disrepair as they were abandoned following secularization in 1834. Some of the buildings disintegrated altogether, while others continued to be used for other purposes. This kitchen at the Carmel mission was restored many years later.

Conclusion

During the 1800s, a few mission churches remained active. San Gabriel was a parish church from 1859 to 1908. San Francisco de Asís remained an active church until the growing city of San Francisco needed a larger one.

Revival and Restoration

Today, the mission at San Antonio de Padua is still owned and run by the Franciscan order.

For the most part, however, the missions were neglected except by a few artists, who painted watercolors or made sketches of the ruins. In the early 1900s, their works began to attract attention. Soon, railroad companies began putting together package tours of the old missions for tourists.

Throughout the twentieth century, various groups in California have restored the missions. Some "restorations" showed little of what the original church looked like. With others, the work was painstaking and took many years, as restorers pored over original plans, old descriptions, and early sketches to recreate the buildings as faithfully as possible.

Today

Today, all the missions have been restored or reconstructed and are open to the public. About two-thirds of the missions are once again owned by the Catholic Church and serve as parish churches, offering regular services.

It is hard to believe when you look at the beautiful and peaceful courtyard of San Juan Capistrano that the missions were once places of such misery.

Two of the missions—San Francisco de Solano and La Purísima Concepción—are now California state historical parks. La Purísima was carefully reconstructed in the 1930s; not only the church but also many of the support buildings, including living quarters and workshops, have been rebuilt. Here, a visitor can learn a great deal about life in the missions of California.

The Legacy of the California Missions

The mission period was a time when huge changes began taking hold in California. Chief among these was the change from Native American cultures to a European way of life. The mission friars did not fully succeed in their aim of converting Native people to live like the Spanish, but they did establish Spanish dominance in the area.

Of course, one reason that Spanish culture gained this foothold was the tragic devastation of the Native American population. There were other reasons as well. The missions fostered the first widespread, European-style farming in the state and introduced cattle ranching and sheep herding. In the late 1840s, English-speaking settlers began entering the state in huge numbers, overwhelming the few Hispanics who lived in California. Still, the cultural seeds planted by the Spanish missions sank roots that are still producing blooms today in the Spanish- and Mexican-influenced architecture, language, food, religion, music, art, and economic life of the state.

Time Line

1542	Juan Rodríguez Cabrillo claims California for Spain.
1602	Sebastían Vizcaíno sails along the California coast, making note of the harbors of San Diego and Monterey.
1769	Don Gaspár de Portolá and Father Junípero Serra lead an expedition to settle California and found the first mission, San Diego de Alcalá, and first presidio at San Diego.
1770	Mission San Carlos de Borroméo de Carmel and the Monterey presidio are founded at Monterey.
1771–1782	Seven more missions are founded under Serra's leadership.
1784	Father Serra dies.
1785	Father Fermín Francisco de Lasuén is named to head the California missions.
1812	Earthquakes damage several missions and destroy San Juan Capistrano.
1821	Mexico gains independence from Spain, and California becomes a Mexican province.
1823	Last mission, San Francisco de Solano, is founded.
1824	Chumash Indians revolt and seize missions of Santa Inés and La Purísima Concepción.
1826	First plan for gradual secularization of missions is announced.
1833	Second plan for gradual secularization.
1834	Mexican government orders immediate secularization of missions.
1857	Mission Santa Cruz is destroyed by an earthquake.
1868	Mission San José is destroyed by an earthquake.
1879	Restoration work begins at Mission San Fernando, Rey de España.
1926	Mission Santa Clara de Asís is destroyed by an electrical fire.
1941	Restoration of La Purísima Concepción is completed.
1982–1985	San José becomes the last mission to be reconstructed or restored.

Glossary

adobe: building material made of mud mixed with straw and dried in the sun.

colony: settlement, area, or country owned or controlled by another nation.

economy: system of producing and distributing goods and services.

empire: political power that controls large territory, usually consisting of colonies or other nations.

friar: member of a Catholic religious order who takes vows of poverty, chastity, and devotion to God's work.

mission: complex built to establish Spanish settlement and serve as center for converting and exploiting the labor of Native Americans who lived in the American Southwest and California.

obsidian: black, shiny, volcanic rock that is as sharp as glass and is useful for forming cutting edges.

peninsula: piece of land jutting out into water but connected to the mainland on one side.

presidio: fort built by Spanish colonialists in the Americas.

prospector: person who explores an area looking for mineral resources such as gold or oil.

province: district of a nation that usually has its own capital town and some form of local government, similar to a state in the United States.

pueblo: Spanish word for town.

resources: useful things, especially naturally occurring materials such as plants, wood, or gold, that can be used, traded, or sold.

scurvy: disease, resulting from a lack of vitamin C in the diet, that causes soft gums, loose teeth, and bleeding.

secularize: make non-religious.

stocks: device for punishing people. A person's head and hands are placed through holes in a wooden structure and locked into place. The person is then left for a long period of time.

stucco: mixture of cement, sand, and powdered limestone used to cover walls.

subjugation: the bringing under control of, or taking power over, one group or person by another group or person.

tallow: animal fat—usually taken from cattle, sheep, or horses—used to make candles or soap.

thatch: dried grasses tied together to make roofing material.

Further Information

Books

Campbell, Paul. *Survival Skills of Native California*. Gibbs Smith, 1999.

Ingram, Scott. *California, the Golden State.* (World Almanac Library of the States). World Almanac Library, 2002.

Nelson, Libby. *Projects and Layouts: California Missions*. Lerner Publications, 1997.

Rawls, James J. *Never Turn Back: Father Serra's Mission* (Stories of America). Raintree Steck-Vaughn, 1993.

Young, Robert. *A Personal Tour of La Purísima* (How It Was). Lerner Publications, 1999.

Web Sites

www.ca-missions.org Large archive about the California Missions with excellent information and links.

library.thinkquest.org/3615/ Information about California missions, including a tour of a typical mission, and the people who lived in them. A web site created by high school students.

www.notfrisco.com/almanac/missions/ Vintage photographs of all the California missions together with extensive historical information on each and a collection of historical documents, such as journals of the mission friars.

Useful Addresses

La Purísima Mission State Historic Park
California State Parks
2295 Purísima Road
Lompoc, CA 93436
Telephone: (805) 733-3713

Carmel Mission Basilica
Rio Road and Lasuén Drive,
Carmel, CA 93921
Telephone: (831) 624-3600

Index

Page numbers in *italics* indicate maps and diagrams. Page numbers in **bold** indicate other illustrations.